I HOPE THIS IS A HAPPY BOOK

Journey Brown-Saintel

BookLeaf Publishing

India | USA | UK

Presentation by *BookLeaf Publishing*

Web: www.bookleafpub.com

E-mail: info@bookleafpub.com

ISBN: 9789358739046

First edition 2021

1. THE MANTRA OF MAKE-IT

Breathe in.

And out.

And in-

Hold-

Now slowly…

Out.

Let it out.

Let it all out:

Scream

Out into the wind

Let it catch on a current

And fly from your lungs.

Cry.

Quiet

In hiding

Or in loud bursts.

Just–

Make it through.

Do anything

And everything

You can do

To make it

through.

2. COLORING BOOK

I made a coloring book today.

Only it wasn't a book

And I ran out of color.

So I took a Black Sharpie

And scribbled a scrappy

Scrubby

Scrambled

Thought bubble

Mumble jumble

Across my kitchen floor.

And my living room walls

And the ceiling in my bedroom.

Today I made a coloring book.

Only I made my own pictures

And went outside the lines

Through the grapevines

Over the cliff

And pushed my stale state

Into it.

Do you wanna but my coloring book today?

5°¡¡§™°¡™§°

Cents.

5 cents on Amazon today.

I tried to click the cents key

And I clicked Alt + BOOM instead.

Do you not have a BOOM key?

What model are you using?

I can you make you one-

Sketch you one—

Draw you one—

In my coloring book today.

Today

I'm going to color

In my coloring book.

Across it.

Outside it.

In between lines

And over the back cover.

Under webs

The kind for spiders

And the kind for liars, too.

And I'll show it you

And you

And you, too

And all of you

And you

And you, too

Will look me and my

Marker of Permanent

In the eye

And say

"Color me

Impressed."

3. STATIC

Sometimes I feel like not everything's going to be okay.

It doesn't matter if it's a Tuesday

Or a happy afternoon

Or if the tea tastes good today

Or if there's a rerun of my favorite show.

My life's like that

(Sometimes.)

((A lot.))

A show, I mean.

Like The Fosters

And Pretty Little Liars

And Blackish

All in one.

An

A

B

C

Show, then.

A

F

R

E

E

F

O

R

M.

But yeah.

Sometimes it drags

Like the letters in that stanza

Hanging right above.

And sometimes

(Often.)

((Always.))

It royally

Sucks.

4. BLANK SPACE

Hey, I missed this day.

Do me a favor?

Grab your own pen

(You own Marker of Permanent)

and jot one in my place.

5. MESS UP

Prefix of Germanic origin

Affixed to nouns and verbs

And meaning "bad, wrong,"

From Old English mis-,

From Proto-Germanic *missa- "divergent, astray"

Productive as word-forming element in Old English

(as in mislæran "to give bad advice, teach amiss")

Word-forming element of Latin origin

(in mischief, miscreant, misadventure, misnomer, etc.),

 From Old French mes- "bad, badly, wrong, wrongly,"

From Vulgar Latin *minus-,

From Latin minus "less"

There's a hundred ways

And a handful of origins

To the root of a

Mistake.

6. INSATIABLE

I'm always hungry.

Deep in my stomach

At the bottom of the cavern

Empty

Pitles

No matter how much

Waste I've consumed

No matter how many

Feet have fallen

Off the edge.

Busy.

I'm always

Always

Busy.

Deep in my email

Clunky inboxes

Steady drafts

Evites and invites and let-me-OUT-vites

Dying.

I'm always always always--

Maybe that's why I'm so hungry.

It's certainly why I'm so busy.

If I cut down my multi-tasking

I'll have too much

Time.

Too much time to think

And feel

And die

(Too much think-to-die

Too much feel-to-die)

So I have to chug along.

7. (WELL, JUST DON'T GET OVERWHELMED.)

My ANXIETY creeps INSIDE uh-me

makes it HARD to breath

WORDS come OVER me

feelslikei'msomebody else—

(Well, just don't get overwhelmed.)

Do you ever get lyrics

stuck

stuck

stuck

in your head?

(Well, just don't get overwhelmed.)

8. SIGN OF THE TIMES

Missing out

Falling behind

Stuck in rewind

(Well, just don't get over—)

Skip. Skip. Skip ahead.

Careful

you might

wind up dead.

Buried beneath

The avalanche—

WARNING: LOOK OUT FOR FALLING ROCKS

WARNING: FALLING ROCKS AHEAD

9. INTERLUDE

I don't want this book to be sad.

I don't remember what I wrote

(B4)

I don't know what I will write

(NXT)

All I know is

(NOW)

I have a choice.

Two roads diverge

(And all that Jazz)

But maybe

(May Bee bzz bzz bzzt)

The choice

Was never

Mine.

Hard hat on

Then

Eyes ahead

Let's see if I

wind

up

dead.

10.

Do you ever want something so bad you could cry?

11. AMBIDEXTROUS

One earbud in

One earbud out

A single ear active

In case of a shout

One canal open

Eardrum bare

Fully aware

A single ear active

(Reactive)

Retractive:

Another ear (attractive)

Clogged w/ rubber and wire

A tunnel vision

Of symphony

12. 11:11

Quick, make a wish.

(And don't say World Peace.)

((I already wished for that.))

Come on.

Still thinking?

Clock is ticking.

You don't have to tell me.

Think

Think

Think

((Tik. Tik. Tik.)

Think

Of it like a candle

On a birthday cake

So quick

(But infinite)

((But *infinite*))

11:12

13. MISC. THOUGHTS

How does a cloud form over a child?

Were they born with it?

Nature vs. Nurture

How can someone be so full of life

So full

Floating on air

Like a balloon

And then burst the next day

The next hour

The next minute

Where did it all go?

((The difference between you and me,

is that when *you* wake up

your nightmare ends.))

Fairest flower

Of the season

I would give my heart

and soul

to you.

((It so easy to pick a flower.

So easy.

But it's not easy for the flower.

(((No, never easy for the flower)))

As soon as you pick it

It dies.))

14. CHANGE IN PERSPECTIVE

The world will never change

and I find it hard to believe that

you can be yourself

I bet this may come as a surprise to you, but

"Who cares what people think?"

is a stupid saying, and

I think that, "Thin is in."

I will let the world know

that it will always be a close-minded place and

society tells me

I have my priorities straight because

what I think

will never be as important as

what others think

I just want you to know that

Celebrities always say they don't care

when it comes to beauty on the outside

Beauty on the inside is more important.

Which is a lie

it's the outside that counts.

there's so many people that say

I seriously need to smile more

how can I?

everyone else is so judgemental

I try so hard to lighten the mood when

I smile and

the whole world turns on me and

when I think society can't get any worse

stuff happens, okay?

the world will always be a terrible place

so, it's ridiculous to believe that

people can change

yet, it's stupid not to think that

the world is extremely terrifying.

And all of this will come true unless we choose to reverse it .

15. THE CAPACITY TO DREAM

Try to imagine

The color

Clexaphonia.

You have never seen it before.

It is not a mixture of

Two colors. Or

Three colors,

It is simply

A new color.

You can't imagine it,

Can you?

Then how are we

To fathom

The idea of space not existing?

What was before space?

A blank canvas.

Well,

then what was before

The blank canvas?

And how

Did

That blank canvas

Come to be?

Can we fathom that?

No.

Not if we don't even

Have the capacity

To imagine

A new color.

16. HEY, CAN WE STOP IDOLIZING WHITENESS?

I know it's hard

Because it's our connotation of brightness

And lightness

Perfect shade and perfect sight—let's

Talk about the gray area on the silver screen

Let's talk about Hollywood's version

Of a Black Queen.

Yo, can we stop idolizing whiteness?

I know it's hard,

Because light skin and loose curls

Makes Zendaya the representation

Of all little black girls.

It's not just an American disease

Can we look at Asia please?

Light skin is not contained to Hollywood

Light skin makes you the face of Bollywood

The face of Thailand

The ideal beauty in each country

On any island

Whether it's your land or my land

Hey, can we stop idolizing whiteness?

Even in our own communities

Colorism isn't just a word

For doodling as you please.

Colorism means

That a little girl with charcoal in her skin

Can be surrounded by sisters and brothers

Who still won't let her in

Despite the fact that whites would say they all have the same
skin

She is abandoned by other Blacks

For she is a shade darker

You see,

Her brownness his starker

And apparently

That makes her other

And not "We."

Because even in the Black community,

We idolize lightness.

Don't be mistaken,

It means we idolize whiteness.

Don't even get me started on LGBT

Apparently

Some of us haven't heard of the word

Intersectionality.

They're fine fighting for the right to love

Amongst accusations of sin

But turn their backs on those fighting for the right to live

Amongst accusations of skin.

Last year the Senate ruled that you can not fire someone

On the basis of who they love.

You're welcome LGBT

That Civil Rights Act fit like a glove.

That's the Act that Blacks in the 60s marched for

That my grandmother set the bar for.

I'm black and I'm gay and I'm calling on you:

The white gays pretending they don't have a clue,

You make me sick

Don't you ever forget

that a Black trans woman threw that first brick.

Can we stop idolizing whiteness?

It's ink-stained in every book I pick up—

Every script that I get—

Reminding that Black is a trait to regret.

Pure

Bright

Light

White

It's ingrained into the English language, see?

Darkness

Scary

Dreary

Dangerous

My own language was made to strangle me.

Search for similes to dark

and you'll see what I mean.

Connotations are demoralizing

And were systematically meant to be seen.

The words we use

are a tool to abuse.

I am black.

I am blackmail.

I am dark.

I am dark comedy.

Dark comedy

Also known as

Black comedy

Also known as

 black humor

Also known as

 dark humor

Also known as

gallows humor.

Need I remind you what a gallow is?

When I said that the English language was meant to strangle
me

I was not being a poet.

Connotations are in every word I write

I forcibly show it.

So, can we stop idolizing whiteness?

Because that's just the first step, guys.

We can't rebuild systems

With bright stars in our eyes.

Light stars in our eyes.

White stars in our eyes.

On our screens.

Behind the scenes—

Yes:

White people are beautiful.

But have you seen gleams

Of ombre, and shades and colorful sheens.

Maybe you haven't because they're not on your screens

Or in the perfect pages of your magazines

Or maybe you have

But

you don't understand what I mean

Because all that you've seen

Is the media depicting color as a two-toned machine

Where light is beauty and dark is obscene—

Fuck that.

If you really want to see something beautiful—

Let's stop idolizing whiteness.

And scene.

17. TIGER, TIGER

Tiger, Tiger, in my view,

the one, the only, braveheart true-

with snarling smile of pearlescent glare-

and wild heart volting magnum cares-

massive paws of delicate touch-

embossed with onyx radiance,

instruct me in taming fears astray,

or don't you quiver when horrors prey?

Tiger, Tiger, in my view,

the one, the only, braveheart true.

18. THE HEADLINE: I SEE YOU.

What does it mean to be seen?

Serene.

Proud of your gleam

Unembarrassed by your stream

Out there

Up stage

In the scene

Front page

Main cover

The Magazine

Why does it mean to dream?

Of what you can be

And not diminish your goals

By what you don't see

In the toy aisles

Or on the TV

But what does it mean to

Dream

With your eyes wide open

To see

Tones that echo your tones

Strands of dead molecules

That twist and turn

And tangle

And stretch

Into the sky like yours do

To see

That THAT person--

That person looks like ME

And they are not hurt

They are not the villain

The bad guy

They are the President

They are HERE

Not just in Rwanda

They are the kings and queens

Of Wakanda

They are powerful.

They are smiling.

They are healthy

And happy

And good

And joyful.

What does it mean

To see Black joy

Unfiltered

In focus

Longer

Than a snapshot.

An album

A gallery

An exhibit

A museum

A monument

Stitched into Earth

Unshakable

Unmovable

With the knowledge

That even if it shakes

Even if it breaks

It will pull itself back together

And carry on

And open its mouth to the heavens

And laugh.

Not a masked laugh,

Not a clown

Nor cartoon

But a laugh filled with the joy of its ancestors

And the excitement of its descents.

How does that feel?

Can you feel that?

Bubbling in your tummy

Shooting, surging into you from the clouds.

That's laughter, baby doll.

That's joy.

The Blackest joy one can find.

Baked like beans

Corny like bread

Homegrown,

Stewed

Cooked in passion, and perseverance

And served up to you.

So take it.

Take a bite.

When you're not busy fighting wars

And saving lives

And crying from stings of systematic

Beehives.

Eat.

This joy is for you.

They tried to hide it from you,

They tried to take it as their own,

But there tongues are twisted

They didn't like the taste

They couldn't consume it

And you damn well know yt people can't season their own food no how,

So how do they look trying to season yours?

It's yours.

Eat.

And don't you let

Anyone

Yuck your yum.

19. SCRITCH, SCRITCH, SCRITCH

My pleasure lies in poetry,

In the freedom to express,

To paint across the visual campus

Etched into the minds of waiting

Drums

Ear drums

Ricocheting

With my truth

Beating in time

With the heart beat

I share.

I am realigning…

My truth

My identity;

Our truth,

Our identity

And the way we share, thrive, survive, and jive

Within our melting pot.

20. READING

Reading is the dusty atlas that guides you through life.

Reading tells you what you must tell others

 and what others might mean

 by what they tell you.

Reading is the torn dictionary flipping through words

and meanings and languages.

Reading is reading

the word reading and reading

to find the meaning of the word

reading.